Linking IEPs to State Learning Standards

Linking IEPs to State Learning Standards

A Step-by-Step Guide

Lynda Miller
Lauren Hoffman

pro·ed
An International Publisher
8700 Shoal Creek Boulevard
Austin, Texas 78757-6897
800/897-3202 Fax 800/397-7633
www.proedinc.com

pro·ed
An International Publisher

8700 Shoal Creek Boulevard
Austin, Texas 78757-6897
800/897-3202 Fax 800/397-7633
www.proedinc.com

Library of Congress Cataloging-in-Publication Data

Miller, Lynda.
Linking IEPs to state learning standards : a step-by-step guide / Lynda Miller and Lauren Hoffman.
p. cm.
Includes bibliographical references and index.
ISBN 0-89-79-884-2 (alk. paper)
1. Individualized education programs—United States. 2. Handicapped children—Education—Standards—United States. I. Hoffman, Lauren. II. Title.
LC4031.M55 2002
371.9'04394—dc21 2001048150

This books is designed in Goudy, Futura, Futura Condensed, and Tekton.

Printed in the United States of America

2 3 4 5 6 7 8 9 10 06 05 04

Contents

Preface

Linking IEPs to State Learning Standards was developed to address the IDEA mandate to link students' Individualized Education Programs with state learning standards. Although almost all 50 states have created drafts or final versions of learning standards, few have developed the supports and procedures necessary to ensure that those standards are used to design students' IEPs. We hope this guide will assist school-based personnel in dealing with the challenges presented by connecting IEPs to state learning standards. We also hope this guide will help teachers who are trying to align their students' education with the general curriculum. The major features of this guide include

- background information regarding state learning standards and their relationship to students' IEPs;
- relevant rules and regulations from the 1997 IDEA statute;
- step-by-step procedures for becoming familiar with state learning standards, discovering how curriculum is related to those standards, and designing IEPs based on standards;
- examples showing how to use this step-by-step process effectively and efficiently; and
- helpful resources for practitioners.

This project significantly benefited from the contributions of several people, to whom we wish to extend our most sincere thanks for their generosity in sharing their experience and expertise about linking IEPs to state learning standards. Leonard Burrello thoughtfully arranged for us to meet with several people in Vermont who had worked tirelessly toward making the connection between state learning standards and writing IEPs. Edie Beatty of Vermont's Teacher Quality Enhancement Project (TQEP) provided an overview of the process of basing IEPs on learning standards. In addition, by using her extensive knowledge of Vermont's educational endeavors, Edie made it possible for us to spend time with several people whose sharing of information and expertise significantly shaped this book. In Vermont, Claudine Prairie, Staff Associate at TQEP, taught us how Vermont's learning standards are applied in the classroom and how rubrics are used in a variety of assessment contexts. Also, Claudine introduced us to Nancy Schiok and Michael Hock, two educators devoted to using learning standards as a means of supporting and teaching students. Nancy's philosophy is evident in the standards-based IEP she developed for her middle school students. She has allowed us to use it as a basis for the IEP described in Appendix C. Michael gave us the materials he uses around the country in his workshops, in which he teaches teachers how to put together IEPs linked to learning standards. Also, his work on rubrics sharpened our own creativity in designing ways to assess student and program progress.

Thanks to Christy Chambers, Director of the Lockport Area Special Education Cooperative, who provided Lauren the time needed to complete this project. We both appreciate her clear recognition that *all* students benefit from being connected to general education.

Special thanks to Jim Patton, editor non pareil, who guided our conceptualization of this manual and who has been a staunch supporter through many projects.

Introduction

The Individuals with Disabilities Education Act Amendments of 1997 (IDEA) charge state education agencies with assuring that IEPs for students with disabilities include performance goals and standards consistent with those established for all children in the state. In other words, the IEP must show how the student is expected to progress toward achievement of each of the state's learning and performance standards. Almost every state has established, or is in the process of establishing, a set of learning standards for its general education curriculum and state- and district-wide assessment programs designed to show how students are progressing toward those standards. Furthermore, the IDEA amendments indicate that performance goals and standards for children with disabilities must be ". . . consistent with other goals and standards for children established by the State" (Hock, 2000a). Hock argues that IEPs that "promote high expectations and access to the general education curriculum" take their focus from state learning standards and from the assessments related to those standards (p. 208). Hock (2000a, 2000b) believes that linking IEPs to standards and assessments yields superior IEPs for the following reasons:

- *Content* standards show how the student is progressing in the acquisition of the skills and knowledge needed to become a useful and productive citizen.
- *Performance* standards provide crucial developmental information, which can be used to predict long term success for the student.
- IEPs linked to state standards explicitly state how the student's learning is related to the real world of living inside and outside the school community.
- Standards-referenced or standards-based IEPs tie the IEP to what is going on in the classroom.
- Standards-referenced or standards-based IEPs promote inclusive education for students with disabilities.
- Standards-referenced or standards-based IEPs provide program consistency between classrooms, schools, and districts.

While the primary purpose of state efforts to develop standards of learning is to raise academic performance for all learners, one of the consequences has been the focus on learner-centered classrooms and schools. The learner-centered perspective couples two ideas. First, learning can be described in terms of components, processes, outcomes, and performances, as exemplified by state learning and performance standards. Second, individual learners possess a unique set of learning needs, talents, interests, backgrounds, capacities, and potentials; these unique sets of needs require teaching practices that best support high levels of student motivation, learning, and achievement (McCombs & Whisler, 1997). We believe that linking the IEP with state learning standards is the best way to ensure that educators address the particular needs of students requiring special education services.

In the following steps, we will guide you through the process of linking student IEPs to your state's learning standards and performance objectives. As you start, keep in mind that content standards and performance objectives are virtually identical with the annual goals and short term objectives used on traditional IEPs, though the nature of those goals and objectives may change once you link them to learning standards and performance objectives.

Step 1: Getting To Know and Understand the Student and Family

Step 2: Getting To Know and Understand Our State's Learning Standards and Performance Goals

Step 3: Getting To Know and Understand Our Local General Education Curriculum and Assessment Plan

Step 4: Getting To Know the Process of Linking District Curriculum with Our State's Learning Standards

Step 5: Getting To Know How To Develop an IEP To Meet 1997 IDEA Requirements

Step 6: Writing Goals To Support Progress Toward the Standard

Step 7: How Do We Link Standards and Students' Needs?

Step 8: Writing Objectives and Benchmarks To Support Progress Toward the Goal

Step 9: Completing an Action Plan

Step 10: Putting Everything Together in an IEP

Step 11: Evaluating Student Progress Toward IEP Goals

Step 12: Monitoring Student Changes Resulting from Standards-Based Learning Goals

Step 13: Evaluating the Plan and the Process

The definitions in Box I.1 will assist you through the linking process.

HELPFUL DEFINITIONS

Standards

- statements of criteria against which comparison can be made
- may be exemplars or criteria to measure the quantity or quality of something
- often established for the purpose of bettering an existing situation
- often tend to be value statements about what is considered important

Content Standards

- broad descriptors of the knowledge students should have as a result of exposure to the curriculum in each standards-setting area
- include important concepts, ideas, issues, and dilemmas in a discipline
- include skills such as thinking, analyzing, communicating, and reasoning

Performance Standards

- concrete, specific examples of what students have to be able to do to demonstrate proficiency in content standards
- describe the nature and quality of student performance that must be demonstrated to be considered acceptable
- define how good is good enough

(*continues*)

Box I.1.

Opportunity To Learn Standards

- define the conditions of teaching and learning that establish the basis for achieving high content and performance standards
- define how schools and districts provide learning access to students
- define school and district responsibility for learning outcomes

Assessment Standards

- provide guidelines for measuring and testing after content and performance standards are developed
- define various means for determining how students are progressing toward content and performance standards

Rubrics

- means for measuring student progress toward standards
- usually consist of
  —a fixed measurement scale (e.g., 4 or 5 points)
  —criteria accompanying each point on the scale
  —sample responses (anchors or benchmarks) illustrating various performance levels

Box I.1. *Continued.*

Getting To Know and Understand the Student and Family: What Are Their Strengths, Needs, and Visions of the Student's Future?

STEP 1

Q How can we learn the family's hopes for this student?

A In our experience, the best way to discover this information is to ask the family in a face-to-face meeting; if this is not possible, through a note sent to the family. Things to ask include the following:

- What do you think are your child's greatest strengths?
- What kinds of things does your child learn most easily?
- What do you think your child would be best at doing as an adult?
- What are your hopes for your child this year?
- What are your hopes for your child by the end of her or his school years?

Q How can we discover the student's learning strengths?

A Ask the student's classroom teachers, peers, and family members what they believe to be the student's learning strengths. Include the following questions:

- What does the child learn most easily at home? At school?
- What does the child most like to do in class? At home?
- What most motivates the child at school? At home?
- What is the child curious about at home? At school?
- What does the child most often choose to do during free time at home? At school?

A Survey existing information about the student:

- Current test data
- Portfolio assessment information
- Classroom performance records
- Recent IEPs
- Team members' observations

A Administer or develop a learning-strengths checklist or profile. Some examples include the following:

- *The Quick Smart Profile for Kids* (Miller & Miller, 1996)
- *The Quick Smart Profile* for adolescents (Miller & Miller, 1994)
- *Multiple Assessments for Multiple Intelligences* (3rd edition) (Chapman, 2000)
- *7 Kinds of Smart: Identifying and Developing Your Many Intelligences* (Armstrong, 1993)

Q How should we address the student's current learning needs, given the information we have collected?

A Describe the following on the IEP:

- Rank order of support needed
- Current levels of classroom performance
- For school-age students, how the student's disability affects her or his involvement and progress in the general curriculum
- For preschoolers, how her or his disability affects involvement in appropriate activities

Getting To Know and Understand Our State's Learning Standards and Performance Goals: What Are the Emphasis and Structure of the Standards?

STEP 2

Q What are the most common ways for state learning standards and performance goals to be written and organized?

A The most common organizational patterns are as follows:

- Content Area
- Fields of Knowledge
- Learner Objectives
- Performance Objectives
- Learning Benchmarks
- Essential Skills Standards

Q What are the characteristics of these organizational patterns?

A Content Area Characteristics

- Organized by subject matter (e.g., English Language Arts and Reading, Mathematics, Social Sciences, Health Education, Physical Education, Economics).
- Typically categorized by grade level and school category such as elementary, middle school, and high school
- Often subcategorized by individual course title, such as "Practical Writing Skills," "Speech Communication," or "Oral Interpretation"

A Fields of Knowledge Characteristics

- Organized by domains of thought (e.g., Arts, Language, and Literature; Science, Mathematics, and Technology; or History and Social Sciences)
- Often subcategorized by themes of learning related to the larger domain of thought. For example, Vermont organized its Arts, Language, and Literature standards into the following six subcategories:

  —Critical Response

  —Literature and Media

  —The English Language

  —Non–Native Language

  —Artistic Process

  —Elements, Forms, and Techniques in the Arts

A Learner Objectives Characteristics

- Organized according to learner outcomes. For example, one of California's math standards requires students to communicate precisely about quantities, logical relationships, and unknown values through the use of signs, symbols, models, graphs, and mathematical terms" (www.cde.ra.gov/board/).
- Often linked to grade levels
- Often linked to content or discipline areas (e.g., California's mathematics standards for Grades 8 through 12: algebra, geometry, and so on)
- Sometimes organized by "strands" (e.g., California's mathematics standards are described in terms of five strands for kindergarten through Grade 7)

A Performance Objectives Characteristics

- Most often described as abilities students should demonstrate at various grade levels
- Often linked to content areas (e.g., Language Arts, Science, Social Studies, Mathematics)

A Essential Skills Standards Characteristics

- Organized according to skills believed crucial to students' success, such as Vermont's Vital Results Standards (www.state.vt.us/educ):

  —Communication Standards

  —Reasoning and Problem Solving Standards

  —Personal Development Standards

  —Civic/Social Responsibility Standards
- Often differentiated into subcategories, such as Vermont's Reasoning and Problem Solving Standards (www.state.vt.us/educ):

  —Questioning

  —Problem Solving

  —Abstract and Creative Thinking
- Often delineated as specific skills across grade level. For instance, in Problem Solving, students in Grades 5 through 8 in Vermont are expected to

  —Seek information from reliable sources, including knowledge, observation, and trying things out;

  —Evaluate approaches for effectiveness and make adjustments;

  —Consider, test, and justify more than one solution;

  —Find meanings in patterns and connections; and

  —Select and apply appropriate methods, tools, and strategies.

Q How are the following terms usually used?

- standards-based
- benchmarks
- goals
- objectives

A **Standards-based** IEPs begin with selecting existing learning standards from the state or district and using them as the base from which to design the student's IEP, including the development of appropriate content, instruction, and assessments related to the selected standards.

A **Goals** set the direction for instruction and assist in determining specific courses, experiences, and skills a student will need to reach his or her vision.

- There is a direct relationship between the goal and the needs identified in the present level of performance.
- Goals are descriptions of what a student can reasonably be expected to accomplish in a 12-month period with the provision of special services.
- A well-written goal is meaningful, measurable, able to be monitored, and useful in making decisions.

A **Benchmarks** are major milestones which specify skill or performance levels a student needs to accomplish to reach his or her annual goal.

- Benchmarks, or short-term objectives (see below), are used on the IEP with the student's annual goal.
- Benchmarks represent the actual content or performance the student is to accomplish at a specific interval or grade level.
- IEP benchmarks should not be confused with the standards or benchmarks school districts have identified for school improvement.

A **Short-term objectives** are used on the IEP with the student's annual goal.

- Short-term objectives are measurable, intermediate steps between a student's present level of performance and the annual goals established for the student.
- The development of short-term objectives is based on a logical breakdown of the major components of the annual goals.
- Short-term objectives measure progress toward the student's annual goals.

Q How are our district's learning standards and performance goals written and organized?

A Complete the Learning Standards/Performance Goals form (see Form 2.1).

LEARNING STANDARDS/PERFORMANCE GOALS

1. Our learning standards/performance goals are organized according to the following (check the ones that apply):

   Content area __________

   Fields of knowledge __________

   Learner objectives __________

   Performance objectives __________

   Learning benchmarks __________

   Essential skills standards __________

2. Our learning standards/performance goals emphasize the following (check the ones that apply):

   Broad concepts __________

   Narrow skills __________

   Grade levels __________

3. Our learning standards/performance goals lend themselves to some degree of interpretation and modification.

   If yes, explain how. ____

   ____

   ____

   If no, explain what this means for your team:

   ____

   ____

   ____

4. We need to better understand the following terminology as it is written in our learning standards/performance goals:

   ____

   ____

   Resources and references that will facilitate our team's learning process:

   ____

   ____

   ____

   ____

   ____

   ____

   ____

Form 2.1.

Getting To Know and Understand Our Local General Education Curriculum and Assessment Plan: What Is the Emphasis?

STEP 3

Q How does our district address the primary purpose of education?

A At its best, education is a moral and intellectual endeavor, always focusing on students and their intentions and needs. However, many schools are more attentive to the technical aspects of schooling than to the ethical aspects.

A By asking how your district curriculum addresses the following issues, you will see how it attends to the ethical aspects of education.

- Putting energy into seeking students' strengths rather than their deficits
- Continuing to foster hope and optimism about the future and potential of our students
- Supporting students' understanding of social responsibility and citizenship
- Supporting students' being active acquirers of learning
- Providing an education that builds bridges and expands students' potential for independence
- Cultivating students' imagination
- Challenging students' thinking with questions and assisting them in seeing multiple possibilities

Q How can we focus our curriculum on students' primary educational needs?

A Create a clear tie between what to teach and the purpose of education by answering the following questions as you design IEPs:

- Is the curriculum flexible?
- Is the curriculum rooted in large questions relevant to students' lives?
- Can classroom discussions lend themselves to diverse viewpoints?
- Are there interconnections between disciplines?
- Is social service expected of students?
- Is student decision making encouraged?
- Is there an emphasis on breadth (compared with depth) of knowledge?
- Is there an emphasis on understanding and critical thinking?
- Is the curriculum prescriptive?
- Do teams have room for decision making regarding what is taught?
- How is our local curriculum aligned with our state's learning standards?

Q What are some guiding characteristics of a Curriculum and Assessment Plan that link it to learning standards?

A We suggest that you refer to the framework in Table 3.1.

TABLE 3.1
Characteristics of Curriculum and Assessment Plans Linked with Learning Standards

Characteristic	Description
Explicit	Expresses clear targets for learning drawn from the identified standards.
Challenging	Organizes content (concepts, skills, and processes) to show increasingly rigorous expectations as students move to higher grades.
Dynamic	Supports rich interactions among the standards, learner strengths and needs, effective instruction, and multidimensional assessment.
Practical	Provides a clear, well-organized, user-friendly format.
Comprehensive	Incorporates all subject areas that are part of the curriculum and emphasizes interconnections between the disciplines.
Cohesive	Uses consistent organizational approaches and language across subject areas throughout the document.
Manageable	Represents not only what all students can learn but also considers the individual needs of students.

Note. Adapted from *Process of Standard Linking*, by Center for Curriculum Renewal, 1999, Burlington, VT: Author. Copyright 1999 by the Center for Curriculum Renewal. Adapted with permission.

Getting To Know the Process of Linking District Curriculum with Our State's Learning Standards: What Steps Can We Take?

STEP 4

Q Where do we begin the process of linking our local curriculum to our state's learning standards?

A The process begins with the following questions:

- Who is currently teaching which standards?
- What is the nature of the instruction?
- Who is currently assessing what standards? By what means? (Carr & Harris, 2001)

Q How is this different from curriculum mapping?

A Curriculum mapping focuses on who is teaching what topics, what materials are used, and what redundancies or overlaps occur within the curriculum

A A process that focuses on linking standards emphasizes who is teaching which standards, how standards are implemented in instruction, and how assessment of the standards occurs.

Q Is there an overall process for linking standards?

A Using the Process of Standards Linking (see Table 4.1) leads to a comprehensive standards-based approach and system.

Q What is alignment and how is it related to linking curriculum to standards?

A Alignment is the process of connecting educational goals, curriculum, instruction, and assessment so that they are consistent with each other and further the same educational purpose(s).

Q How do we determine if our district's curriculum is aligned with our state's learning standards?

A Query the district's curriculum office to determine any curriculum alignment initiatives.

A Examine each curriculum area and look at goals to see if they are matched.

A Obtain any district publications relating to alignment (i.e., look for publications from taskforces, committees, departments).

A Peruse the state's education Web site and compare it with our district's site, looking for evidence of alignment.

Q If our district's curriculum is NOT aligned with our state's standards, how can we begin the alignment process?

A Complete the Curriculum Mapping form (see Form 4.1) to show student work as it actually happens in the classroom and in relation to state and district standards (Jacobs, 1997).

TABLE 4.1

The Process of Standards Linking

The following are the eleven components of standards linking. Keep in mind that the process of standards linking is recursive, and that the list indicates the logical relationship of the components rather than the order in which the process should proceed.

- **Vision**

  What are the standards, evidence, and learning opportunities to which the school or district is committed?

- **Current State**

  Who is currently teaching which standards and evidence?

  What is the nature of the instruction?

  Who is currently assessing which standards and evidence? By what means?

- **Curriculum and Assessment Plan**

  Who is responsible for teaching which standards and evidence?

  What should instruction look like?

  What is to be assessed? By whom? By what means?

- **School Decisions**

  Through which courses, topics, and themes will the standards be taught and assessed?

  Do all students have opportunities to be instructed and assessed in relation to the standards?

- **Resources**

  What is needed in the way of funding, expertise, and materials?

- **Professional Development Plan**

  What do teachers need to know and be able to do in order to teach and assess?

  How will opportunities to address these needs be provided over time?

- **Supervision and Evaluation**

  What supports and feedback will teachers receive as they work to implement the curriculum?

  Who is responsible for providing what?

  What documentation is needed?

- **Student Profile**

  What assessment information will be kept on each student, K–12?

- **Comprehensive Assessment System**

  How will the local curriculum be assessed?

  What sources of data will be included?

- **Reporting**

  What information is needed by which audiences?

  How will it be provided?

- **Action Plan**

  What do we need to do to improve student learning?

Note. Adapted from *Process of Standards Linking*, by the Center for Curriculum Renewal, 1999, Burlington, VT: Author. Copyright 1999 by the Center for Curriculum Renewal. Adapted with permission.

CURRICULUM MAPPING

Phase 1: Each teacher collects data about what she or he actually teaches

1. Describe the processes and skills emphasized in your classroom.

____

____

____

2. Describe the curriculum content in terms of essential concepts and topics as examined in essential questions.

____

____

____

3. Describe the products and performances produced during the assessments of learning in your classroom.

____

____

____

Phase 2: Individual teacher examination of collected maps

1. List any repetitions or gaps you found in comparing each teacher's curriculum description from Phase 1.

____

____

____

2. Describe any assessments that seemed particularly meaningful to you.

____

____

____

3. Describe how you can reduce any unwanted redundancies across the curriculum.

____

____

____

4. Describe curricular aspects you found that matched your district's or state's learning standards.

____

____

____

(continues)

Form 4.1.

CURRICULUM MAPPING *Continued.*

Phase 3: Mixed groups of faculty members report on their findings

1. Select a facilitator for this process.

2. Each teacher reports her or his findings from individual reviews of the curriculum maps. This process does not involve making any decisions or judgments about curriculum or curriculum maps.

3. Each facilitator summarizes her or his group's findings.

4. Facilitators meet to select a facilitator for the large group review (Phase 4) and to summarize the small group findings in a chart showing each reporting session.

5. Facilitators distribute the chart to all faculty members.

Phase 4: Faculty members review mixed group reports

1. Facilitator solicits and lists faculty members' comments on emerging patterns.

(continues)

Form 4.1. *Continued.*

CURRICULUM MAPPING *Continued.*

Phase 5: Faculty members determine immediate and long-term goals for curriculum revision

1. Facilitator assists faculty members in determining areas that can be handled by individual faculty members, teams, or administrators.

2. Facilitator assists faculty members in determining which areas can be addressed immediately.

3. Facilitator assists faculty members in determining which areas need further, in-depth research before a solution can be produced.

Phase 6: Faculty members determine a schedule for the curriculum review cycle

1. Facilitator and faculty members determine a curriculum review schedule and format for the remainder of the school year.

   Schedule

   Format

Form 4.1. *Continued.*

Getting To Know How To Develop an IEP To Meet 1997 IDEA Requirements: What Are the Guidelines for Writing Goals, Objectives, and Benchmarks?

STEP 5

Q What are the necessary (i.e., mandated) components of the IEP?

A Table 5.1 shows what must be included in the IEP under IDEA 1997—Section 614(d)(1)(A). (See also Appendix A, which includes a fuller description of the IDEA rules and regulations.)

TABLE 5.1

What Must Be Included in the IEP under IDEA 1997—Section 614(D)(1)(A)

1. Present Levels of Performance.
   A statement of the child's present level of educational performance, including
   - how the child's disability affects her or his involvement and progress in the general curriculum; and
   - for preschool children, as appropriate, how the disability affects the child's participation in appropriate activities.
2. Measurable Annual Goals, Including Benchmarks or Short-term Objectives.
   A statement related to
   - meeting the child's needs resulting from his or her disability to enable the child to be involved in and progress in the general curriculum; and
   - meeting each of the child's other educational needs that result from the child's disability.
3. Special Education and related services, supplementary aids and services to be provided to the child, or on behalf of the child, and the program modifications or supports for school personnel.
   A statement showing what will be provided for the child to
   - advance appropriately toward attaining the annual goals;
   - be involved in and progress in the general curriculum and participate in extracurricular and other nonacademic activities; and
   - be educated with and participate with other children with disabilities and nondisabled children in extracurricular and other nonacademic activities.
4. An explanation of the extent, if any, to which the child will not participate with nondisabled children in the regular class and in extracurricular and other nonacademic activities.
5. A statement of any individual modifications in the administration of state- or district-wide assessments that are needed in order for the child to participate in such assessments.

(continues)

- If the IEP team determines that the child will *not* participate in a particular state- or district-wide assessment of student achievement, they must provide
  - a statement of why that assessment is not appropriate for the child, and
  - a statement of how the child will be assessed.

6. Services, dates, and timelines:
   - projected date for the beginning of the services and modifications described in special education and related services and in supplementary aids and services, and in program modifications or supports; and
   - the anticipated frequency, location, and duration of those services and modifications.
7. A statement describing transition plans:
   - beginning at age 14 and updated annually, a statement of the transition service needs of the child under the components of the child's IEP that focus on the child's courses of study;
   - beginning at age 16, or younger if appropriate, a statement of needed transition services for the child, including, when appropriate, a statement of the interagency responsibilities or any needed linkages; and
   - beginning at least one year before the child reaches the age of majority, a statement that the child has been informed of rights under this title, if any, that will transfer to the child on reaching the age of majority.
8. A statement of progress toward annual goals:
   - how the child's progress toward the annual goals will be measured;
   - how the child's parents will be regularly informed (which must be at least as often as parents of nondisabled children are informed) of their child's progress toward the annual goals and the extent to which that progress is sufficient to enable the child to achieve the goals by the end of the year.

Q How can our team develop the IEP so that it includes the mandated components?

A Complete the IEP Development Checklist (see Form 5.1 on the following pages):

IEP DEVELOPMENT CHECKLIST

Present Levels of Performance

1. Describe the student's strengths.

____

____

____

2. Describe the student's needs, preferences, and interests.

____

____

____

3. Describe the student's and parents' hopes, dreams, and goals for postschool activities.

____

____

____

4. Describe how the student's performance in each area of the general curriculum compares to state- or district-established standards.

____

____

____

5. Describe what curricular/instructional strategies have been effective with the student.

____

____

____

6. Describe what curricular/instructional strategies have *not* been effective with the student.

____

____

____

7. In what courses, activities, or settings does the student need assistance?

____

____

____

8. Describe the assistance needed for the student in those courses, activites, and settings.

____

____

(*continues*)

Form 5.1.

IEP DEVELOPMENT CHECKLIST *Continued.*

Measurable Annual Goals, Including Benchmarks or Short-Term Objectives

Given the student's strengths, hopes, dreams, and goals for his or her future and his or her present levels of performance:

1. Describe the yearlong goals and the benchmarks (i.e., short-term objectives) related to the general curriculum that will help the student work toward his or her hopes and dreams.

   ____

   ____

   ____

2. Describe the yearlong goals and the benchmarks (i.e., short-term objectives) outside the general curriculum that will help the student work toward his or her hopes and dreams.

   ____

   ____

   ____

3. Describe how we will know whether the student is making progress toward these goals and benchmarks.

   ____

   ____

   ____

As soon as students reach age 14 (no later) and every year thereafter:

4. Describe how the measurable goals and the benchmarks (i.e., short-term objectives) are consistent with the course of study decisions made by the IEP team.

   ____

   ____

   ____

No later than age 16 (younger if appropriate) and every year thereafter:

5. Describe how the measurable goals and the benchmarks (i.e., short-term objectives) are consistent with the IEP team's decisions regarding transition services needed to help the student achieve his or her postschool dreams and goals.

   ____

   ____

   ____

   ____

   ____

   ____

(continues)

Form 5.1. *Continued.*

IEP DEVELOPMENT CHECKLIST *Continued.*

Special Education and Related Services, Supplementary Aids and Services, and Program Modifications and Supports

1. What assistance (beyond that which is made available to all students in the general education environment) does this student need, and what program modifications and supports must be provided to school personnel so that the student can do the following:

Assistance to Student	**Program Modifications/ Supports Provided to School Personnel**

A. Make appropriate progress in the general curriculum, consistent with the student's annual goals?

B. Make appropriate progress toward meeting each of the student's other annual goals?

C. Participate in extracurricular and other nonacademic activities?

D. Be educated and participate with other children with disabilities and nondisabled children in extracurricular and other nonacademic activities?

(continues)

Form 5.1. *Continued.*

IEP DEVELOPMENT CHECKLIST *Continued.*

2. Beginning no later than age 14, and every year thereafter, describe the services that must be included in the student's IEP related to her or his transition service needs and to ensure that she or he progresses in appropriate courses of study, as determined by the IEP team.

___

___

___

3. Beginning at age 16 (or younger if appropriate) and every year thereafter, describe the services that must be included in the student's IEP related to needed transition services to help the student achieve his or her postschool dreams and goals.

___

___

___

Participation with Nondisabled Children in the Regular Classroom and in Extracurricular and Other Nonacademic Activities

1. What parts of the day can the student participate with nondisabled children in the regular classroom and in extracurricular and other nonacademic activities?

___

___

___

2. What supplementary aids and services are needed to enable the student to participate effectively in the regular classroom and in extracurricular and other nonacademic activities?

___

___

___

3. What parts of the day can the student not participate with nondisabled children in the regular classroom and in extracurricular and other nonacademic activities?

___

___

___

Participation in District- and State-wide Assessments

1. Describe the types of modifications that are in place for the student during instruction, demonstration, and mastery in the regular classroom.

___

___

___

(continues)

Form 5.1. *Continued.*

IEP DEVELOPMENT CHECKLIST *Continued.*

2. Are those same modifications necessary and appropriate in order for the student to demonstrate knowledge and skills in the district- or state-wide assessments? Yes _____ No______

   If not, describe why not.

   ____

   ____

   ____

3. What, if any, additional modifications or accommodations are necessary and appropriate in the administration of district- or state-wide assessments? Describe them.

   ____

   ____

   ____

4. If it is not appropriate for the student to participate even with modifications or accommodations, describe why not.

   ____

   ____

   ____

5. If it is not appropriate for the student to participate in all parts of an assessment, even with modifications or accommodations, describe how the student could appropriately participate in parts of the assessment.

   ____

   ____

   ____

6. If it is not possible to participate in any part of a given assessment, even with modifications and accommodations, describe how the student will be assessed.

   ____

   ____

   ____

Services, Dates, and Timelines

For each special education or related service, supplementary aid or service, and program modification or support described in the student's IEP, what is our procedure for answering the following questions:

1. When will it begin?
2. How often will it be provided?
3. Where will it be provided?
4. For how long will it be provided?

   ____

   ____

   ____

(*continues*)

Form 5.1. *Continued.*

5. If we do not have an existing procedure, how can we create one?

____

____

____

Transition

1. How have we ensured that the student understands the extent to which parental rights under Part B will transfer to him or her on reaching the age of majority?

____

____

____

2. Is the student linked to any needed postschool services, programs, or supports before the student exits school? If so, describe them.

____

____

____

3. If not, describe why the student is not linked to these services, programs, or supports.

____

____

____

Progress Toward Annual Goals

1. Describe how we will measure the student's progress toward the annual goals.

____

____

____

2. Is the student's progress likely to enable the student to achieve the goals by the end of the year?
   Yes ______ No______

   If no, describe why not.

____

____

____

(*continues*)

IEP DEVELOPMENT CHECKLIST *Continued.*

3. Describe what the IEP team will do if it is unlikely the student will achieve the annual goals by the end of the year.

____

____

____

4. Who will inform the student and the parents of the student's progress toward the annual goals?

____

____

____

5. Describe how we will inform the student and his or her parents of the student's progress toward the annual goals at least as often as parents of students without disabilities are informed.

____

____

____

Form 5.1. *Continued.*

Writing Goals To Support Progress Toward the Standard: What Goals Will Assist the Student in Achieving the Selected Learning Standards?

STEP 6

Q How can our state's learning standards be used to foster a learning-focused, customized, results-oriented approach to education?

A With Reigeluth's (1997) "Using Learning Standards To Design IEPs" as a guide, (see Box 6.1), follow the steps below:

USING LEARNING STANDARDS TO DESIGN IEPS

- Standards should be used as levels of attainment, with many different levels in each area of competence.
- Standards should be used without timetables; that is, standards should not be tied to age levels or time. Some standards may be common in the sense that all students should eventually attain them, but no standards should be common in the sense that all students should be required to attain them at the same age.
- Standards should be used in all areas of learning and human development—nonacademic and academic standards can be effective only if they represent what parents, employers, educators, and community members believe children should learn and be able to do.
- Within limits, there should be choice in selecting standards—teachers, parents, and students should be allowed to decide when a given standard is appropriate (challenging yet attainable) for a child during the child's development.
- Standards should be accompanied by learning-focused instructional processes. Standards must be supported by instructional processes that allow children to continue to work on the attainment of a standard until it is reached. Teachers need to be coaches and mentors, and they need to use team-based learning, problem-based learning, differentiated instruction, and technology as tools for customizing learning.

Box 6.1. *Note*. Adapted from "Educational Standards: To Standardize or to Customize Learning?" by C. Reigeluth, 1997, *Phi Delta Kappan*, *74*(3), 202–206.

1. List which learning standards apply to this student.

____

____

____

2. Reword the learning standards listed in number 1 to reflect levels of attainment appropriate for this student.

____

____

____

3. For each learning standard, first eliminate any timetables for attainment, then describe the steps toward attainment that this student is most likely to successfully take.

___

___

___

4. Describe the standards this student will be expected to meet in areas not covered by your state's learning standards (i.e., any nonacademic areas pertinent to this student).

___

___

___

5. Describe who will be responsible for helping the student attain any learning standards not specified in your state's learning standards.

___

___

___

6. Describe the process you will use to ensure that teachers, parents, and students can challenge the appropriateness or suitability of any learning standard that has been selected for this student.

___

___

___

7. Describe how instruction will be designed and customized so that this student meets the selected learning standards (i.e., team-based learning, problem-based learning, differentiated instruction, technology).

___

___

___

Box 6.2 shows suggestions for linking IEP goals, objectives, and benchmarks to learning standards.

LINKING IEP GOALS, OBJECTIVES, AND BENCHMARKS TO LEARNING STANDARDS

Choosing Appropriate Standards for the Student

- Use the same content standard you use for the other students in the classroom or grade.
- Modify the performance standard or level to fit this student's need, or choose a prerequisite standard that leads to this content standard.
- If there is no appropriate standard for younger students or students with severe disabilities, begin with standards aimed at helping this student gain access to the learning opportunities available in the classroom.
- For older students, consider selecting performance standards from a lower level (e.g., 4th grade writing or language arts standards for an 8th grader).
- Consider developing a subset of a particular performance standard (e.g., for a standard addressing sounds, syllables, and letter patterns, you could generate a subsidiary standard, such as "recognizes one- and two-syllable words.").

Writing Goals, Objectives, and Benchmarks Linked to Standards

- Use the standard as it is written, adding particulars for this student (e.g., Sarah will make progress toward meeting *Kentucky Goal 1: Use Basic Communication and Mathematics Skills, Academic Expectation 1:2 :Students make sense of the variety of materials they read.* Materials and activities include Sarah telling the story in a wordless picture book using an Initiating Event, an Attempt, and a Consequence.

Box 6.2. *Note.* Adapted from *Standards, Assessments, and IEPs: Planning for Success in the General Education Curriculum*, by M. Hock, 2000, Burlington: Vermont Department of Education.

How Do We Link Standards with Student Needs?

STEP 7

In Box 7.1, you will see selected examples of standards from two states. We chose these examples because more than 90% of IEPs have goals related to communication, reading, and writing (Hock, 2000a).

EXAMPLES OF STANDARDS FROM TWO STATES

Kentucky's Learning Goals and Academic Expectations

1. Students are able to use basic communication and mathematics skills for purposes and situations they will encounter throughout their lives.

1.1	Students use reference tools such as dictionaries, almanacs, encyclopedias, and computer reference programs and reserach tools such as interviews and surveys to find the information they need to meet specific demands, explore interests, or solve specific problems.
1.2	Students make sense of the variety of materials they read.
1.3	Students make sense of the various things they observe.
1.4	Students make sense of the various messages to which they listen.
1.5–1.9	Students use mathematical ideas and procedures to communicate, reason, and solve problems.
1.10	Students organize information through development and use of classification rules and systems.
1.11	Students write using appropriate forms, conventions, and styles to communicate ideas and information to different audiences for different purposes.
1.12	Students speak using appropriate forms, conventions, and styles to communicate ideas and information to different audiences for different purposes.
1.13	Students make sense of ideas and communicate ideas with the visual arts.
1.14	Students make sense of ideas and communicate ideas with music.
1.15	Students make sense of ideas and communicate ideas with movement.
1.16	Students use computers and other kinds of technology to collect, organize, and communicate information and ideas

(continues)

Box 7.1. *Note*. From *Kentucky Learning Goals and Academic Expectations*, by Kentucky Department of Education, 2000, Frankfort: Kentucky Department of Education [Online]. Available: www.kde.state.ky.us/oapd/curric/Publications/Transformations/acadex.htm; *Vermont Framework of Standards*, by Vermont Deartment of Education [Online]. Available: http://www.state.vt.us/educ/stand/framework.htm

Vermont Framework of Standards

1. Communications Standards
   Writing
   Personal Essays

   1.12 In personal essays, students make connections between experiences and ideas. This is evident when students:

PreK–4	a	Reflect on personal experience, or the experience of an imagined character, using patterns of cause/effect, comparison, and classification.
5–12	aa	Relate personal experiences to concepts, patterns, and ideas.
5–12	b	Trace the process of reflection, making connections between thoughts and experience; and
5–12	c	Establish a commonplace, concrete occasion as a context for reflection.
9–12	d	Maintain a thoughtful voice and style.

Box 7.1. *Continued.*

1. Identify the learning standards we have chosen for the student.

   ____
   ____
   ____

2. Identify the accomodations, modifications, or supplementary aids and services the student will require to meet the learning standard.

   ____
   ____
   ____

3. Identify the program supports and services needed for school personnel to implement the IEP.

   ____
   ____
   ____

4. Identify the learning standards and performance objectives most relevant to this student's needs.

   ____
   ____
   ____

5. Resolve any discrepancies between #1 and #4.

   ____
   ____
   ____

1. What assistance (beyond that which is made available to all students in the general education environment) does this student need, and what program modifications and supports must be provided to school personnel so that the student can do the following:

Assistance to Student	**Program Modifications/ Supports Provided to School Personnel**

A. Make appropriate progress in the general curriculum, consistent with the student's annual goals?

Assistance to Student	Program Modifications/Supports Provided to School Personnel
Provide Sara continual visual/verbal modeling and feedback regarding her turn-taking skills.	Provide classroom teachers with materials to enhance Sara's turn-taking skills.
Provide Sara with pictorial descriptions of the expectations of classroom directions and work.	Provide teachers with exemplars of pictorial descriptions of directions.
Provide Sara with scaffoldings during her communicative turns in the classroom.	Provide a short training session on how to scaffold turn taking for Sara.

B. Make appropriate progress toward meeting each of the student's other annual goals?

Assistance to Student	Program Modifications/Supports Provided to School Personnel
Allow Sara more time to complete assignments.	Provide consultation regarding how to allow more time for Sara to complete assignments and how to reduce the number of assignments she is expected to complete.
Reduce the number of assignments Sara is expected to complete.	
Provide Sara with instructional materials that include explanatory visuals.	Provide teachers with exemplars of alternative materials that incorporate explanatory visuals.

C. Participate in extracurricular and other nonacademic activities?

Assistance to Student	Program Modifications/Supports Provided to School Personnel
Provide Sara with opportunities to role-play communication in nonacademic and extracurricular activities.	Provide Sara's teachers with training in role-playing communicative turn taking with Sara.
Inform Sara's family about the activities available for her to participate in.	Provide time for Sara's teachers to consult with her family.
Consult with adult leaders of nonacademic activities regarding Sara's communication.	Provide adult leaders of nonacademic activities information about Sara's communication needs.

D. Be educated and participate with other children with disabilities and nondisabled children in extracurricular and other nonacademic activities?

Assistance to Student	Program Modifications/Supports Provided to School Personnel
Address transportation needs to make certain Sara can participate in nonacademic activities.	Provide ongoing inservice and training for teachers to ensure they have the information and knowledge they need to assist Sara.
Encourage Sara to participate in nonacademic activities (e.g., Girl Scouts).	Provide administrative support for school personnel to assist Sara (e.g., release time, funding, transportation).
Encourage her parents in their efforts to provide nonacademic activities for Sara.	

Figure 7.1. Example of completed student assistance and program modifications form.

Writing Objectives and Benchmarks To Support Progress Toward the Goal: What Objectives and Benchmarks Will Assist the Student in Achieving the Goals?

STEP 8

Q How do we write the annual goals and short-term objectives linked to standards or performance goals?

A Using the descriptions you generated in the lists completed in Steps 6 and 7, respond to the following items (Box 8.1 provides an example):

Gathering Information for the IEP

1. Using the information you gathered in Step 6, where you identified modifications and accomodations for this student, describe the most appropriate learning standards for this student.

   ____

   ____

   ____

2. Prioritize these learning standards for this student.

   ____

   ____

   ____

3. Describe how the learning standards you have selected will be modified, if necessary, for this student.

   ____

   ____

   ____

4. Write annual goals that address this student's movement toward competence in the learning standard (i.e., avoid simply stating the standard). Box 8.1 illustrates numbers 4, 5, and 6 using one of Minnesota's content standards for English language arts.

   ____

   ____

   ____

5. Based on the annual goals you described in number 4, write short-term objectives for this student (see Sara's IEP in Figure 10.1 in Step 10).

____

____

____

6. Describe progress indicators for this student in realistic, measurable, and attainable terms (see Sara's IEP in Figure 10.1 in Step 10).

____

____

____

EXAMPLE OF ANNUAL GOAL, SHORT-TERM OBJECTIVES, AND PERFORMANCE INDICATORS BASED ON A LEARNING STANDARD

The Pertinent Learning Standard

Minnesota Content Standard 4: All students will use the English language effectively.

Short-Term Objectives

1. Student will demonstrate awareness of differences in language patterns used in spoken, written, and visual communication contexts, such as the home, playground, classroom, and storybook.
2. Student will become aware of and begin to experiment with different ways to express the same idea.

The Annual Goals

1. Student will develop awareness of the differences in language patterns used in spoken communication contexts, especially at school.
2. Student will begin to experiment with different ways to use language to express ideas.

The Performance Indicators

Shares information and increases conversational interactions with others.

Uses effective voice and tone.

Constructively expresses preferences, feelings, and needs.

Uses language to express needs.

Box 8.1.

Completing an Action Plan: What Still Needs To Be Identified or Explored by the Educational Team?

STEP 9

Q What was missing or incomplete as you completed Steps 1 through 8?

A Respond to the following queries:

1. For **Step 1,** what were you unable to complete or what did you identify as missing about the student's and family's hopes and vision? Describe it.

____

____

____

Describe what your team plans to do to remedy this situation.

____

____

____

2. Follow the same procedure for **Step 2.** For example, could you find the state standards? What information were you unable to provide when filling out the Learning Standards/Performance Goals checklist? Describe what was missing.

____

____

____

Describe the remedies you have designed.

____

____

____

3. Follow the same procedure for **Step 3.** Describe what was missing and the remedies you designed.

____

____

____

4. Follow the same procedure for **Step 4.** Describe what was missing and the remedies you designed.

____

____

____

5. Follow the same procedure for **Step 5.** Describe what was missing and the remedies you designed.

____

____

____

6. Follow the same procedures for **Step 6.** Describe what was missing and the remedies you designed.

____

____

____

7. Follow the same procedures for **Step 7.** Describe what was missing and the remedies you designed.

____

____

____

8. Follow the same procedures for **Step 8.** Describe what was missing and the remedies you designed.

____

____

____

Q We have identified the information and data we need to complete an action plan. How do we develop an action plan?

A An action plan guides you through the process of summarizing where you are in linking IEPs with your district's or state's learning standards, determining what you need to do to comply with the federal regulations mandating the link between IEPs and state learning standards, and developing a reasonable timetable for coming into compliance.

To develop the action plan in this step, you will need the data and information you gathered in Steps 1 through 8 and summarized in the first part of Step 9. Use this information and data to complete the Action Plan (see Form 9.1).

ACTION PLAN

Action Plan for:____________________

Date:____________________

Team Facilitator:____________________

Educational Team Members:____________________

What Needs To Be Done	Who Will Be Responsible	Timeline	Follow-up Plan/Completed

Notes from Discussion:____________________

Form 9.1.

Putting Everything Together in an IEP

STEP 10

Q How can we incorporate the information we have gathered in the preceding steps into a manageable IEP?

A The IEP template in Appendix C incorporates everything we have described in the preceding steps. You can customize the template so that it includes the elements required in your district or state.

A Figure 10.1 shows a standards-based IEP designed for Sara, a 7-year-old student identified as having a language disorder. This is page 3 of the IEP, which describes what we know about the student, what we are going to do to help the student receive an appropriate education, and how we will know if we are succeeding.

INDIVIDUALIZED EDUCATION PROGRAM DESCRIPTION		
What do we know about Sara?	What are we going to do to help Sara receive an appropriate education?	How will we know if we are succeeding?
Sara demonstrates limited awareness of differences in language patterns used in her spoken communication in the school context. Sara answers simple questions when asked by peers and adults; however, she doesn't request information or ask for clarification from others. She doesn't easily take turns in a conversation with her peers and does not attempt to repair her communication attempts when she's unsuccessful in communicating her ideas or needs. She is unsure whether the directions in class are suggestions for completing her work or are step-by-step instructions that must be followed.	Sara will receive classroom-based communication support 60 minutes per week in the general third grade classroom, provided collaboratively by the speech–language pathologist and the classroom teacher. Sara will be provided with the following classroom supports: • Continual visual/verbal modeling and feedback regarding her communication attempts • Continual visual/verbal modeling and feedback regarding her requests for information and clarification • Continual visual/verbal modeling and feedback regarding her turn-taking skills • Use of visual supports and verbal cues to increase her awareness and understanding of the flow of communication • Explicit descriptions of the expectations of classroom directions and work	By June 3, 2001, Sara will visually/verbally signal awareness of the differences in language patterns used in her spoken communication contexts, especially at school, so as to progress toward meeting the Minnesota Content Standard 4 (1): All students will use the English language effectively. Awareness of language differences will be assessed using the Communication Rubric. By Oct. 15, 2000, Sara will score in the "Getting There" category on 2 out of the 4 criteria. By Jan. 13, 2001, Sara will score in the "Getting There" category on all 4 criteria. By April 1, 2001, Sara will score in the "Sometimes" category on 2 out of the 4 criteria. By June 3, 2001, Sara will score in the "Sometimes" category on all 4 criteria.
Include present levels of educational performance, the student's learning strengths, how the student's disability affects her or his involvement and progress in the general curriculum, or, for preschoolers, in appropriate activities.	Include special education and related services, personnel, frequency, duration, location of services, and, if necessary, accommodations, supplementary aids and services, transition services, extracurricular and other nonacademic activities or other services.	Include goals and objectives that cover evaluation procedures, objective criteria, and the expected dates for accomplishment. Goals should lead to the student being involved in and progressing in the general curriculum.

Figure 10.1. Page 3 of a sample IEP form filled out for Sara.

Evaluating Student Progress Toward IEP Goals

STEP
11

Q How can we design assessments that provide optimal opportunities for students to show progress?

A Developing an assessment plan is the best way to ensure that the IEP offers optimal opportunities for the student to demonstrate progress toward learning–standards-derived goals.

An assessment plan is a set of choices showing how student learning will be assessed in relation to the selected learning standards. The plan illustrates various sorts of evidence collected to demonstrate student progress toward the standards and goals and the criteria identified to demonstrate achievement. The assessment plan is a way to ensure that student assessment is conducted through a variety of evaluation and assessment tools, processes, and procedures. The components of an assessment plan are

- the selected learning standards for the student;
- the goals generated for the student, which are based on the selected learning standards;
- a set of activities or experiences, aligned with the standards, designed for the student;
- various sources of evidence through which the student will demonstrate attainment of the identified goals.

According to the Vermont Department of Education (2000), the two types of evidence sources that can be used are (a) constructed responses (short answer, products [e.g., journal, mobile, collage], performances [e.g., oral report, skit, performing a poem]), (b) selected responses (multiple choice, true–false test).

The assessment plan is best developed in tandem with the design of the student's goals, benchmarks, and objectives. Table 11.1 provides definitions, examples, and information related to developing a successful assessment plan.

A Another means for assessing student progress toward IEP goals is the use of rubrics.

A rubric is a set of categories, organized along a simple measurement scale, used to track progress toward a standard, goal, or objective. The categories along the scale typically describe the skills or behaviors needed to meet the standard, goal, or objective, while the measurement scale generally consists of two (e.g., yes/no; can do it/can't do it) to four levels of proficiency (e.g., beginner, novice, proficient, distinguished).

TABLE 11.1
Assessment Planning Guide

	What the Student Produces			
	Selected Response	**Constructed Responses**		
		Short Answers	**Products**	**Performances**
Definition	Student selects from among responses	Items for which the student must create her or his response or answer	Documents or artifacts created by the student	Demonstrations and interactions carried out by the student
Examples	Multiple choice True–False Matching	Fill in the blank: word(s), phrase(s); Short answer: sentence(s), paragraph(s); Label a diagram; "Show your work"; Visual representation: web, concept map, flow chart, graph/table	Essay, research paper, log/journal, lab report, story/play, poem, portfolio, art exhibit, science project, model, video/audio tape, spreadsheet, learning log.	Oral expression, science lab, dance/movement, demonstration, athletic competition, dramatic reading, debate, musical recital, "think aloud."
How the assessment is created and used	Identifies standards and criteria to be assessed; Selects or creates items; Pilots and refines items; Creates and uses scoring guide(s).	Identifies standards and criteria to be assessed; Selects or creates items; Pilots and refines items; Creates and uses scoring guide(s)	Identifies standards and criteria to be assessed; Defines task(s); Reads, observes, questions, interviews	Identifies standards and criteria to be assessed; Defines task(s); Reads, observes, questions, interviews, creates and uses scoring guide(s)
Scoring Guides	Answer key Scoring template Machine scoring	Generalized rubric Task-specific rubric Checklist Answer key	Generalized rubric Task-specific rubric Checklist Answer key	Generalized rubric Task-specific rubric Checklist Observation sheet.
Reporting/ Feedback Methods	Narrative report (oral or written); Checkist; Written comments; Letter grades: Numerical score (percentages, point totals); Verbal report/conference; Developmental/proficiency scale; Generic rubric; Task-specific rubric; Rating scale			
Assessor	Self; Teacher(s); Peer(s); Parent(s); Expert judges; Community members			

Note. Adapted from *Using Standards in Your Classroom: A Teacher Resource Guide*, by D. Snow, N. Pfister, and C. Prairie, 2000, Burlington: Vermont Department of Education.

In general, we followed Hock's steps for formulating rubrics (Hock, 2000b). For example, in developing the Communication Rubric shown in Table 11.2—for a student learning nonverbal and verbal means for expressing herself effectively—we followed this process:

1. Choose a goal: The overall goal measured by this rubric is assessing a student's progress toward meeting her annual goals as described on her IEP.
2. Decide what will be measured to determine progress: We selected four aspects of the student's communication abilities:
   - she shares information and increases conversational interactions with others;
   - uses effective voice and tone;
   - constructively expresses preferences, feelings, and needs; and
   - uses language to express needs.

The learning standard for this particular student is from Kentucky's state learning goals and academic expectations.

Goal 1: *The Student Will Use Basic Communication and Mathematics Skills;* **Academic Expectation 1.12:** *Students speak using appropriate forms, conventions, and styles to communicate ideas and information to different audiences for different purposes.*

The rubric was developed with a timeline showing that by October 30, 2000, the student will fall within the "Getting There" category on 2 out of 3 checkpoints; by January 22, 2001, the student will fall into the "Getting There" category on 3 out of 3 checkpoints; by April 1, 2001, the student will fall into the "Sometimes" category on 1 out of 3 checkpoints; and by June 14, 2001, the student will fall within the "Sometimes" category on 2 out of 3 checkpoints.

TABLE 11.2

Communication Rubric

	Just Learning	Getting There	Sometimes
Shares information and increases conversational interactions with others.	I am beginning to learn how to take turns, stay on a topic, and end a conversation with others.	I am practicing using my conversational skills with other people by role-playing, scripting, and social stories.	I can sometimes take turns, stay on a topic, and end a conversation with others.
Uses effective voice and tone.	Sometimes I forget to use my soft voice to talk.	I can use my soft voice when someone shows me how to show my strong feelings.	I can show strong feelings by using my soft voice without being reminded.
Constructively expresses preferences, feelings, and needs.	Sometimes I forget to use appropriate words and/or actions. Sometimes I call people names. Sometimes I push or hit people.	I have been using friendly and respectful words. I can use friendly body language when an adult reminds me.	I can use friendly and respectful words and body language. I can use words when I'm feeling uncomfortable or angry. I ask adults for help when I'm frustrated.
Uses language to express needs.	Sometimes I forget to use words to ask for what I need. Sometimes I use unfriendly words, actions, or tone of voice.	When an adult reminds me, I can use friendly words to ask for what I need.	I can figure out that I need something without asking an adult. I can use feeling words to say how I feel. I can let adults know what I need.

Note. Copyright 2002 by Lynda Miller and Lauren Hoffman.

Monitoring Student Changes Resulting from Standards-Based Learning Goals

STEP 12

Q How can we determine the effects of using standards-based learning goals on our students' learning and progress?

A In our experience, the best way to learn how using standards-based goals is affecting our students it to obtain feedback from them, and from team members and parents. This feedback can be used to gain a broad perspective of the effects of using standards-based learning goals. We designed the rubric in Table 12.1 with this in mind.

TABLE 12.1

Rubric for Assessing the Impact of Standards-Based Goals

	Just Beginning	Emerging	Sometimes	Always
Purpose and use of Assessment	Standardized and authentic forms of assessment are used.	Standardized and authentic forms of assessment are used in relation to instruction.	Standardized and authentic forms of assessment are used in relation to instruction and learning standards.	Standardized, authentic forms of assessment used in relation to instruction and learning standards; students and families understand and have input into the assessment.
Levels of Support for Students and Families	Support is available if student is unsuccessful and help is requested.	Support is available any time at student request.	Support is built into the most difficult parts of the student's schedule.	Ongoing support is easily accessible and is integrated into all aspects of the student's school schedule.
Stakeholder Involvement	Administrators are primarily responsible for campus-wide planning and decision making.	Information is solicited from teachers in campus-wide planning and decision making.	Teachers and students are a part of campus-wide planning and decision making.	Teachers, students, and families are viewed as a team and have ongoing dialogue and input into campus-wide planning and decision making.
School Climate	Teachers and administrators talk about the need to tolerate individual differences and develop school policy to support this effort.	Teachers and administrators talk about academic and social diversity as a strength to be celebrated.	School and classroom practices support student diversity.	Students and families have a sense of belonging in the school.
Communication	Communication with school staff is available on request.	Communication with school staff occurs in relation to difficult or challenging situations.	Communication with school staff is scheduled periodically throughout the school year.	Communication with teachers and administrators is ongoing and easily accessible throughout the school year.

Evaluating the Plan and the Process: How Effectively Have We Used Standards as a Reference Point for IEPs?

STEP 13

Q How can we determine how effective we are in using learning standards as a reference point for students' IEPs?

A We have developed another rubric for you to use to measure your progress in becoming more effective (see Table 13.1).

We hope that this manual has served not only as a guide in your efforts to link IEPs with state learning standards, but also as a springboard for thoughts about how you want to proceed from here.

TABLE 13.1
Using Learning Standards To Guide IEPs

	Just Beginning	Emerging	Sometimes	Almost Always
Familiar with student's strengths and family's hopes and visions of the student's future.	We agree we need to identify student strengths and family hopes for the student.	We have chosen a means for identifying student's strengths and family's hopes.	Our IEP format includes a place to describe student strengths and family hopes.	Our IEPs describe student strengths and family hopes.
Conversant with our state's learning standards and performance objectives.	We have copies of our state's learning standards readily available	We have identified the learning standards most relevant to the students for whom we are writing IEPs.	We use learning standards to guide goal-writing for some of our students.	Goals on our student's IEPs include goals derived direclty from learning standards.
Know how to link learning standards with student needs.	We have identified the accommodations, modifications, and supplementary aids and services the student will require to meet the learning standard.	We have identified the program supports and services needed for school personnel to implement the IEP.	We have identified the learning standards and performance objectives most relevant to the student's needs.	Students' IEPs indicate how their unique needs will be met in their progress toward the learning standard.
Can write goals linked with standards.	We have selected the learning standards that are relevant for each of our students.	We have identified how each relevant learning standard can be attained by each of our students.	We have described how instruction will be designed and customized for each student.	We write goals reflecting the standards, how they will be attained, and how instruction will be customized.
Can write objectives and benchmarks that assist student in progressing toward goals and standard(s).	We have identified the relevant learning standard(s) for each of our students.	We have prioritized these learning standards for each of our students.	We have described how we will modify (if necessary) or task-analyze each learning standard.	We write objectives and benchmarks consistent with the learning standards selected for each student.

Note. Copyright 2002 by Lynda Miller and Lauren Hoffman.

IDEA 1997 Rules and Regulations

APPENDIX A

12441 Federal Register/Vol. 64, No. 48/ Friday, March 12, 1999/Rules and Regulations

§ 300.346 Development, review, and revision of IEP.

(a) Development of IEP.

(1) General. In developing each child's IEP, the IEP team shall consider—

(i) The strengths of the child and the concerns of the parents for enhancing the education of their child;

(ii) The results of the initial or most recent evaluation of the child; and

(iii) As appropriate, the results of the child's performance on any general State or district-wide assessment programs.

(2) Consideration of special factors. The IEP team also shall—

(i) In the case of a child whose behavior impedes his or her learning or that of others, consider, if appropriate, strategies, including positive behavioral interventions, strategies, and supports to address that behavior;

(ii) In the case of a child with limited English proficiency, consider the language needs of the child as those needs relate to the child's IEP;

(iii) In the case of a child who is blind or visually impaired, provide for instruction in Braille and the use of Braille unless the IEP team determines, after an evaluation of the child's reading and writing skills, needs, and appropriate reading and writing media (including an evaluation of the child's future needs for instruction in Braille or the use of Braille), that instruction in Braille or the use of Braille is not appropriate for the child;

(iv) Consider the communication needs of the child, and in the case of a child who is deaf or hard of hearing, consider the child's language and communication needs, opportunities for direct communications with peers and professional personnel in the child's language and communication mode, academic level, and full range of needs, including opportunities for direct instruction in the child's language and communication mode; and

(v) Consider whether the child requires assistive technology devices and services.

(b) Review and Revision of IEP. In conducting a meeting to review, and, if appropriate, revise a child's IEP, the IEP team shall consider the factors described in paragraph (a) of this section.

(c) Statement in IEP. If, in considering the special factors described in paragraphs (a)(1) and (2) of this section, the IEP team determines that a child needs a particular device or service (including an intervention, accommodation, or other program modification) in order for the child to receive FAPE, the IEP team must include a statement to that effect in the child's IEP.

(d) Requirement with respect to regular education teacher. The regular education teacher of a child with a disability, as a member of the IEP team, must, to the extent appropriate, participate in the development, review, and revision of the child's IEP, including assisting in the determination of—

(1) Appropriate positive behavioral interventions and strategies for the child; and

(2) Supplementary aids and services, program modifications or supports for school personnel that will be provided for the child, consistent with § 300.347 (a)(3).

(e) Construction. Nothing in this section shall be construed to require the IEP team to include information under one component of a child's IEP that is already contained under another component of the child's IEP.
(Authority: 20 U.S.C. 1414(d)(3) and (4)(B)and (e))

§ 300.347 Content of IEP.

(a) **General.** The IEP for each child with a disability must include—

(1) A statement of the child's present levels of educational performance, including—

(i) How the child's disability affects the child's involvement and progress in the general curriculum (i.e., the same curriculum as for nondisabled children); or

(ii) For preschool children, as appropriate, how the disability affects the child's participation in appropriate activities;

(2) A statement of measurable annual goals, including benchmarks or short-term objectives, related to—

(i) Meeting the child's needs that result from the child's disability to enable the child to be involved in and progress in the general curriculum (i.e., the same curriculum as for nondisabled children), or for preschool children, as appropriate, to participate in appropriate activities; and

(ii) Meeting each of the child's other educational needs that result from the child's disability;

(3) A statement of the special education and related services and supplementary aids and services to be provided to the child, or on behalf of the child, and a statement of the program modifications or supports for school personnel that will be provided for the child—

(i) To advance appropriately toward attaining the annual goals;

(ii) To be involved and progress in the general curriculum in accordance with paragraph (a)(1) of this section and to participate in extracurricular and other nonacademic activities; and

(iii) To be educated and participate with other children with disabilities and nondisabled children in the activities described in this section;

(4) An explanation of the extent, if any, to which the child will not participate with nondisabled children in the regular class and in the activities described in paragraph (a)(3) of this section;

(5)(i) A statement of any individual modifications in the administration of State or district-wide assessments of student achievement that are needed in order for the child to participate in the assessment; and

(ii) If the IEP team determines that the child will not participate in a particular State or district-wide assessment of student achievement (or part of an assessment), a statement of—

(A) Why that assessment is not appropriate for the child; and

(B) How the child will be assessed;

(6) The projected date for the beginning of the services and modifications described in paragraph (a)(3) of this section, and the anticipated frequency, location, and duration of those services and modifications; and

(7) A statement of—

(i) How the child's progress toward the annual goals described in paragraph (a)(2) of this section will be measured; and

(ii) How the child's parents will be regularly informed (through such means as periodic report cards), at least as often as parents are informed of their nondisabled children's progress, of—

(A) Their child's progress toward the annual goals; and

(B) The extent to which that progress is sufficient to enable the child to achieve the goals by the end of the year.

(b) **Transition services.** The IEP must include—

(1) For each student with a disability beginning at age 14 (or younger, if determined appropriate by the IEP team), and updated annually, a statement of the transition service needs of the student under the applicable components of the student's IEP that focuses on the student's courses of study (such as participation in advanced-placement courses or a vocational education program); and

(2) For each student beginning at age 16 (or younger, if determined appropriate by the IEP team), a statement of needed transition services for the student, including, if appropriate, a statement of the interagency responsibilities or any needed linkages.

(c) **Transfer of rights.** In a State that transfers rights at the age majority, beginning at least one year before a student reaches the age of majority under State law, the student's IEP must include a statement that the student has been informed of his or her rights under Part B of the Act, if any, that will transfer to the student on reaching the age of majority, consistent with § 300.517.

Resources

APPENDIX B

In this appendix, we have included references to print materials and Web sites we have found useful in our own efforts to link IEPs with learning standards.

Print

Armstrong, T. (1993). *7 kinds of smart: Identifying and developing your many intelligences*. New York: Penguin.

Carr, J. F., & Harris, D. E. (2001). *Succeeding with standards: Linking curriculum, assessment, and action planning*. Alexandria, VA: Association for Supervision and Curriculum Development.

Chapman, C. (2000). *Multiple assessments for multiple intelligences* (3rd edition). Arlington Heights, IL: Skylight.

Hock, M. (2000a). Standards, assessments, and teacher education programs: Planning for success in the general education curriculum. In R. A. Villa & J. S. Thousand (Eds.), *Restructuring for caring and effective education* (pp. 208–241). Baltimore: Brookes.

Hock, M. (2000b). *Standards, assessments, and IEPs: Planning for success in the general education curriculum*. Burlington: Vermont Department of Education Comprehensive System of Personnel Development.

Individuals with Disabilities Education Act Rules and Regulations, 64 Fed. Reg. 12429 (1999).

McCombs, B., & Whisler, J. S. (1997). *The learner-centered classroom in schools: Strategies for increasing student motivation and achievement*. San Francisco: Jossey-Bass.

Miller, L., & Hoffman, L. P. *Linking IEPs to learning standards*. Lockport, IL: Staff Development Workshop.

Miller, L., & Miller, L. C. (1994). *The quick smart profile*. Austin, TX: Smart Alternatives.

Miller, L., & Miller, L. C. (1996). *The quick smart profile for kids*. Austin, TX: Smart Alternatives.

Snow, D., Pfister, N., & Prairie, C. (2000). *Using standards in your classroom: A teacher resource guide*. Burlington: Vermont Department of Public Education.

Web Sites

The Web sites listed in this section were current as of April 1, 2001. If you experience difficulty finding any of these sites, go to the state-level site (e.g., http://www.state.tx.us), follow the links to "Education" (sometimes Education is listed under State Departments and Agencies, Government, Public Instruction or Superintendent of Instruction), and from there follow the links to learning standards, which have different names across sites. Sometimes we found the standards through links to Curriculum or Curriculum and Instruction.

Alaska's Department of Education and Early Development Standards:
http://www.eed.state.ak.us/qschools/standards.html
Alabama Courses of Study Content Standards site—follow the links to Courses of Study (COS) from:
http://www.alsde.edu/html/sections_detail.asp?section=54
Arizona's Academic Standards and Accountability:
http://www.ade.state.az.us/standards/
Arkansas's Learning Standards:
http://arkedu.state.ar.us/standard.htm
California's K–12 Academic Content Standards:
http://www.cde.ca.gov/board/
Colorado's Standards in Action:
http://www.cde.state.co.us/index_action.htm
Connecticut's Common Core of Learning:
http://www.state.ct.us/sde/dtl/curriculum/currkey2.htm
Delaware's Content and Framework Standards:
http://www.doe.state.de.us/DPIServices/DOE_Standards.htm
Florida's Sunshine State Standards:
http://www.firn.edu/doe/curric/prek12/frame2.htm
Georgia's Quality Core Curriculum:
http://www.glc.k12.ga.us/passwd/search/srchqcc/homepg.htm
Hawaii's Implementation of Standards-Based Reform:
http://doe.k12.hi.us/standards.htm
Idaho's Achievement Standards:
http://www.sde.state.id.us/osbe/exstand.htm
Illinois's Learning Standards:
http://www.isbe.state.il.us/ils/default.htm
Indiana's Academic Standards:
http://www.doe.state.in.us/standards/welcome.html
Iowa's Standards Development for School Improvement:
http://www.state.ia.us/educate/standards/weblinks.html
Kansas's Assessments and Standards:
http://www.ksbe.state.ks.us/assessment/index.html
Kentucky's Curriculum Framework:
http://www.kde.state.ky.us/oapd/curric/Publications/Transformations/trans.html
Louisiana's Content Standards:
http://www.doe.state.la.us/DOE/asps/home.asp?I=CONTENT
Maine's Learning Results:
http://www.state.me.us/education/lres/homepage.htm
Maryland's School Performance Program's Content Standards:
http://mdk12.org/mspp/standards/index.html
Massachusetts's Curriculum Frameworks:
http://www.doe.mass.edu/frameworks/default.html

Michigan's Content Standards and Draft Benchmarks:
http://cdp.mde.state.mi.us/mcf/contentstandards/default.html
Minnesota's Graduation Standards:
http://cfl.state.mn.us/GRAD/Intro1.htm
Mississippi's Key Priorities (not yet fully developed standards):
http://www.mde.k12.ms.us/index.htm
Missouri's Show Me Standards (Performance and Knowledge):
http://www.dese.state.mo.us/standards/
Montana's Content and Performance Standards:
http://www.metnet.state.mt.us/SchoolImprovement/HTM/Mtstandards.shtml
Nebraska's Academic Standards:
http://www.nde.state.ne.us/Issu/AcadStand.html
Nevada's New Academic Standards:
http://www.nde.state.nv.us/sca/standards/index.html
New Hampshire's Curriculum Frameworks:
http://www.ed.state.nh.us/CurriculumFrameworks/curricul.htm
New Jersey's Core Curriculum Content Standards and Curriculum Frameworks:
http://www.state.nj.us/njded/cccs/index.html
New York's State Learning Standards:
http://www.nysatl.nysed.gov:80/standards.html
North Carolina's Standard Course of Study:
http://www.ncpublicschools.org/curriculum/
North Dakota's State Standards:
http://www.dpi.state.nd.us/standard/index.shtm
Ohio's Academic Content Standards:
http://www.ode.state.oh.us/ca/ci/acs/acsindex.htm
Oklahoma's Priority Academic Student Skills:
http://sde.state.ok.us/publ/pass.html
Oregon's Teaching and Learning to Standards:
http://www.ode.state.or.us/TchgLrngStds/
Pennsylvania's Proposed Academic Standards:
http://www.pde.psu.edu/standard/stan.html
Rhode Island's Standards, Instruction, and Student Assessment:
http://www.ridoe.net/standards/default.htm
South Carolina's Curriculum Standards:
http://www.sde.state.sc.us/sde/educator/crindex.htm
South Dakota's Content Standards:
http://www.state.sd.us/deca/ContentStandards/index.htm
Tennessee's Curricular Frameworks:
http://www.state.tn.us/education/ci/cicurframwkmain.htm
Texas's Essential Knowledge and Skills (TEKS):
http://www.tea.state.tx.us/teks/
Utah's Core Curriculum:
http://www.uen.org/cgi-bin/websql/utahlink/CoreHome.hts
Vermont's Framework of Standards and Learning Opportunities site—follow the links from:
http://www.state.vt.us/educ/

Virginia's Standards of Learning:
http://www.pen.k12.va.us/VDOE/Instruction/sol.html

Washington's Essential Academic Learning Requirements:
http://www.k12.wa.us/reform/EALR/default.asp

West Virginia's Instructional Goals and Objectives:
http://wvde.state.wv.us/igos/

Wisconsin's Model Academic Standards:
http://www.dpi.state.wi.us/standards/index.html

Wyoming's Content and Performance Standards plan (some standards are online and can be found by using the search engine on the Wyoming Department of Education Home Page at http://www.k12.wy.us/wdehome.html#services. Type in "Content and Performance Standards"): http://www.k12.wy.us/cgi-bin/print_hit_bold.pl/publications/standard.html?content+and+performance#first_hit

IEP Template

Appendix C

Note. Adapted from an IEP developed by Nancy Evans-Shiok. Adapted with permission.

INDIVIDUALIZED EDUCATION PROGRAM (IEP)

IEP Manager: ____________________ IEP Meeting Date: ____________________

Student Name: ____________________ Disability Category: ____________________

Birth Date: ____________________ Student Number: ____________________

Parent/Guardian: ____________________ Grade Assigned: ____________________

Address: ____

Phone: Work: ____________________ Home: ____________________

Individuals at the IEP Meeting

1. **Parent/Guardian**	5. **Transition Planning Participants/Agencies**
Name:	Name:
Relationship to student:	Position:
2. **Regular Education Teacher:**	Name:
Name:	Position:
Position:	
3. **Special Education Teacher or Service Provider:** (check appropriate box)	(Indicate who is responsible for interpreting the instructional implications of evaluation results)
LEA Representative: ☐	Name:
Individual who can interpret the instructional implications of evaluation results: ☐	Position:
Name:	Name:
Position:	Position:
4. **Student:**	Name:
Name:	Position:

Definitions and Comments

Continuum of Placements:

Alternative placements such as instruction in regular classes, special classes, special schools, home instruction, and instruction in hospitals and institutions are available to meet the special education needs of students with disabilities.

Duration of Services:

Special education and related services will be delivered during the school calendar year or on a schedule set in the IEP.

Evaluation Personnel:

An individual who can interpret the instructional implications of evaluation results. This could be the regular or special education teacher, the LEA representative, or another individual.

Goals:

A statement of the measurable annual goals, including benchmarks or short-term objectives, related to meeting the student's needs that result from the student's disability. These goals enable the student to be involved in and progress in the general curriculum.

Individualized Education Program/Accountability:

Each public agency must provide special education and related services to the student with a disability in accordance with an IEP. However, neither state nor federal regulations require that any agency, teacher, or other person be held accountable if a student does not achieve the growth projected in the annual goals and objectives.

Least Restrictive Environment:

Each public agency shall ensure that, to the extent appropriate, students with disabilities, including students in public or private institutions or other care facilities are educated with students who are nondisabled, and that special classes, separate schooling, or other removal of students with disabilities from the regular education environment occurs only if the nature or severity of the disability is such that education in regular classes with the use of supplementary aids and services cannot be achieved satisfactorily.

Local Education Agency (LEA) Representative:

The LEA representative is a representative of the public agency who is knowledgeable about general curriculum, qualified to provide or supervise the provision of special education services, and is knowledgeable about the availability of resources. A public agency may designate another member of the IEP team to serve as the LEA representative if the individual meets the criteria stated above.

Regular Education Teacher:

At least one regular education teacher must participate in the development of the IEP if the student is, or may be, participating in the regular education environment.

Related Services:

Related Services means transportation and such developmental, corrective, and other supportive services as are required to assist a student with a disability to benefit from special education (e.g., OT, PT, parent counseling, etc.)

Skill Areas:

Skill areas include Basic Skill Areas (e.g., reading, communication), Fundamental Skills (e.g., cognitive, social), or any other curriculum areas needed by the student (e.g., vocational, recreational, nonverbal communication). The student's needs for socialization, language, and behavior development must be considered.

Special Education:

Special Education means specially designed instruction, at no cost to the parents, to meet the unique needs of a student with a disability. This includes instruction conducted in the classroom, home, hospitals, institutions, and other settings; and instruction in physical education, travel training, speech–language pathology, and vocational education.

Student:

The student with the disability is encouraged to participate in the development of the IEP whenever appropriate. Starting at age 14, the student is required to be invited when transition service needs or transition services will be discussed.

Transition Services:

Transition Services means a coordinated set of activities designed to promote movement from school to postsecondary activities. Transition services may be special education or related services.

INDIVIDUALIZED EDUCATION PROGRAM DESCRIPTION

What do we know about ________?	What are we going to do to help ____________________ receive an appropriate education?	How will we know if we are succeeding?
Include present levels of educational performance, the student's learning strengths, how the student's disability affects her or his involvement and progress in the general curriculum, or, for preschoolers, in appropriate activities.	Include special education and related services, personnel, frequency, duration, location of services, and, if necessary, accommodations, supplementary aids and services, transition services, extracurricular and other nonacademic activities or other services.	Include goals and objectives that cover evaluation procedures, objective criteria, and the expected dates for accomplishment. Goals should lead to the student being involved in and progressing in the general curriculum.

Required IEP Planning Checklist

Student Name: ____________________ IEP Meeting Date: ____________________

DON'T FORGET: AS YOU COMPLETE THE IEP DOCUMENT, YOU MUST DO THE FOLLOWING:	Done	NA
1. Discuss the applicable section(s) of Parental Rights in Special Education.	☐	
2. Document parent participation if parents were not in attendance.	☐	
3. Record on the cover page the date of initiation and the duration of services.	☐	
4. Plan an adaptive physical education program for those students who cannot participate in the regular physical education program. (Not applicable for early childhood).	☐	☐
5. Consider the related services necessary to assist a student with a disability to benefit from special education and related services. Include transportation, speech–language services, audiology services, psychological services, physical and occupational therapy, recreation, counseling, early identification and assessment of disabilities in students, orientation and mobility services, parent counseling and training, school health services, social work services, and so on.	☐	
6. Describe accomodations needed for the student to participate in state- or district-wide assessments. If the student will not participate in state- or district-wide assessments, describe why the assessment is not appropriate and how the student will be assessed.	☐	☐
7. Include strategies, positive behavioral interventions, and supports to address behavior issues when the behavior interferes with the student's or other students' learning.	☐	☐
8. Consider and include language needs of students with limited English proficiency as they relate to the students' IEP.	☐	☐
9. Provide instruction and materials in Braille for students who are blind or visually impaired. If the IEP team decides not to provide Braille, document the reasons why. This decision must be based on an evaluation of the student's current and future reading and writing skills and media needs.	☐	☐
10. Consider the communication needs of the student.	☐	☐
11. For students who are deaf or hard of hearing, consider the student's language and communication needs, including opportunities for direct communication with peers and professional personnel in the student's language and communication mode. Also include opportunities for direct instruction in the student's language and communication mode.	☐	☐
12. Consider whether the student requires assistive technology devices and services.	☐	☐
13. Consider the extent to which the student can be educated with her or his nondisabled peers. If the IEP team determines that the student cannot participate full time with nondisabled students in the regular classroom, extracurricular or other nonacademic activities, explain why full participation is not possible.	☐	

References

Armstrong, T. (1993). *7 kinds of smart: Identifying and developing your many intelligences*. New York: Penguin.

Carr, J. F., & Harris, D. E. (2001). *Succeeding with standards: Linking curriculum, assessment, and action planning*. Alexandria, VA: Association for Supervision and Curriculum Development.

Center for Curriculum Renewal. (1999). *Process of standards linking*. Burlington, VT: Author.

Chapman, C. (2000). *Multiple assessments for multiple intelligences* (3rd edition). Arlington Heights, IL: Skylight.

Hock, M. (2000a). Standards, assessments, and teacher education programs: Planning for success in the general education curriculum. In J. S. Thousand & R. A. Villa (Eds.), *Restructuring for caring and effective education* (pp. 208–241). Baltimore: Brookes.

Hock, M. (2000b). *Standards, assessments, and IEPs: Planning for success in the general education curriculum*. Burlington: Vermont Department of Education Comprehensive System of Personnel Development.

Individuals with Disabilities Education Act Amendments of 1997, 20 U.S.C. § 1401 (26).

Individuals with Disabilities Education Act Rules and Regulations, 64 Fed. Reg. 12429 (1999).

Jacobs, H. H. (1997). *Mapping the big picture*. Alesxandria, VA: Association for Supervision and Curriculum Development.

McCombs, B., & Whisler, J. S. (1997). *The learner-centered classroom in schools: Strategies for increasing student motivation and achievement*. San Francisco: Jossey-Bass.

Miller, L., & Miller, L. C. (1994). *The quick smart profile*. Austin, TX: Smart Alternatives.

Miller, L., & Miller, L. C. (1996). *The quick smart profile for kids*. Austin, TX: Smart Alternatives.

Reigeluth, C. (1997). Educational standards: To standardize or to customize learning? *Phi Delta Kappan*, *74*(3), 202–206.

Snow, D., Pfister, N., & Prairie, C. (2000). *Using standards in your classroom: A teacher resource guide*. Burlington: Vermont Department of Public Education.

About the Authors

Lynda Miller is president and director of Smart Alternatives, Inc., a company devoted to the development and dissemination of innovative ideas in learning and communication. For over 30 years, Lynda has studied schooling and the most effective practices for enhancing students' learning. Currently she writes and edits books and materials on narrative, learning, intelligence, communication, and school-related issues. Lynda is also a graphic artist specializing in digital art. Her most recent digital art publications are *Two Friends* and *Bird & His Ring*. She lives in Austin, Texas.

Lauren Hoffman is coordinator of The Learning Network at the Lockport Area Special Education Cooperative. The Learning Network is a professional development support system for educators, administrators, parents, students, and community members designed to focus on teaching and learning for all students. Laurie is also currently consulting with school districts in Indiana and Michigan as they transform their special education programs into more unified and collaborative educational systems. Laurie is an adjunct faculty member at Lewis University in Romeoville, Illinois, and teaches coursework on collaboration and consultation. She lives in Schererville, Indiana.